This book belongs to

A letter from mummy

_____

_____

_____

_____

_____

_____

_____

_____

_____

_____

_____

_____

A letter from daddy

Mummy and daddy

A picture of mummy and daddy

How we met_____

_____

Our favourite memory together_____

_____

The funniest thing we went through_____

_____

My family

A picture of my family

I have _____ brothers _____ and sisters.

Their names and ages are _____

_____

_____

_____

_____

Before I was born

Mummy found out she was pregnant when I was_____
_____

What mummy loved to eat while pregnant_____
_____

The first time mummy felt me move_____
While pregnant mummy gained_____

Mummy&daddy's most favourite memories

_____
_____
_____
_____
_____
_____
_____
_____

Before I was born

Place ultrasound photo here

Date_____

Thoughts _____

_____

_____

_____

Before I was born

A photo of mummy while pregnant

Mummy's thoughts while pregnant _____

_____

_____

_____

_____

_____

Before I was born

A photo of mummy while pregnant

Funniest memories while pregnant _____

_____

_____

_____

_____

_____

_____

_____

My baby shower

Place photo here

Date _____

People present on that day _____

_____

_____

_____

The gifts I received on that day _____

_____

_____

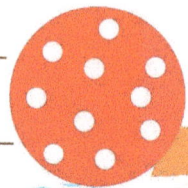

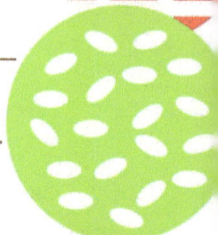

My baby shower

Place photo here

Special memories and thoughts on that day_____

_____

_____

_____

_____

_____

_____

_____

A letter from mummy

A letter from daddy

_____

_____

_____

_____

_____

_____

_____

_____

_____

_____

_____

_____

_____

_____

My arrival

How I was delivered_____

The doctor who delivered me_____

Place of delivery_____

Time of delivery_____

The first person to carry me_____

The person who cut my umbilical cord_____

The people present on that day_____

_____

_____

_____

My special characteristics_____

_____

_____

_____

_____

My arrival

The first real picture of me

How mummy and daddy felt when they first saw me _____

_____

_____

_____

_____

_____

My arrival

My name is _____

My family chose this special name because _____

_____

The meaning of my name is _____

_____

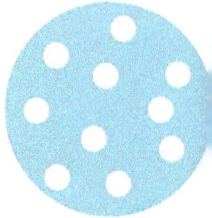

Funny nicknames my family used to call me:

_____

_____

_____

_____

_____

My arrival

My tiny handprint

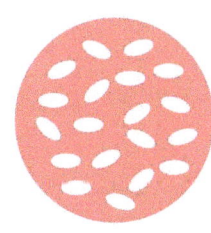

My tiny footprint

My arrival

A photo of me and mummy

Thoughts_____

_____

_____

_____

_____

My arrival

A photo of me and daddy

Date _____

Thoughts _____

_____

_____

_____

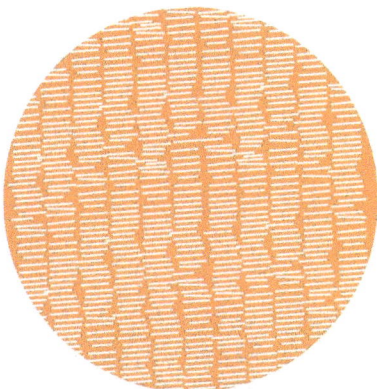
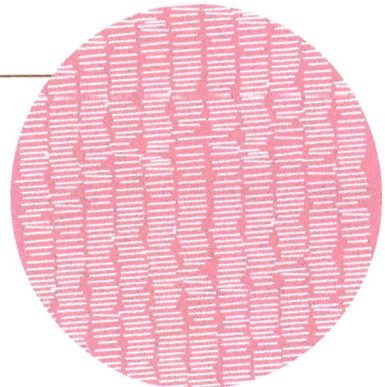

Welcome home

I came home when I was _____ days old.

The address of my first home was_____

_____

I was welcomed at home by_____

_____

How mummy and daddy felt when I first came home

_____

_____

_____

_____

What I did the first week at home_____

_____

_____

_____

_____

_____

_____

Welcome home

Place photo here

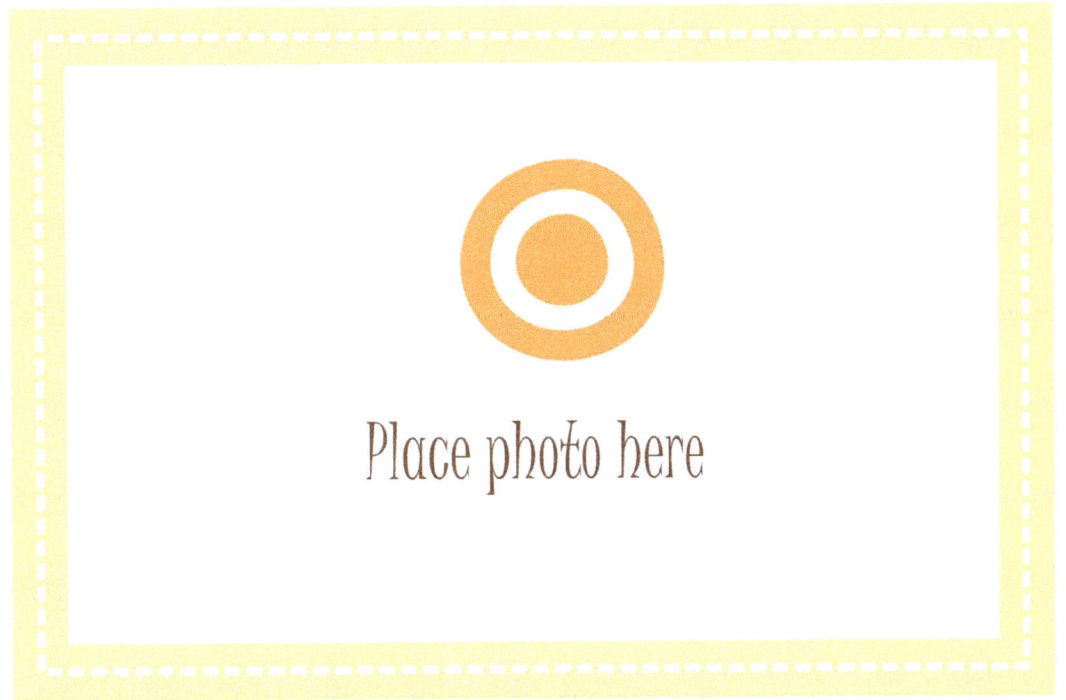

Place photo here

Welcome home

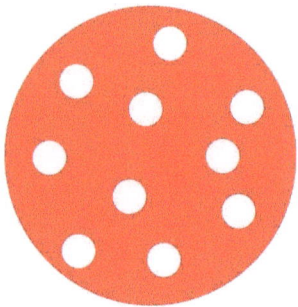

Place photo here

Place photo here

Welcome home

Place photo here

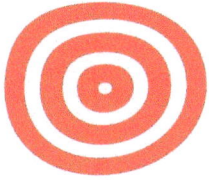

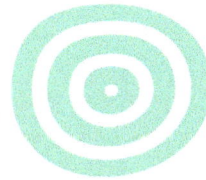

Place photo here

Watch me grow

Date	Age	Weight	Height
_____	1 month	_____	_____
_____	2 months	_____	_____
_____	3 months	_____	_____
_____	4 month	_____	_____
_____	5 months	_____	_____
_____	6 months	_____	_____
_____	7 month	_____	_____
_____	8 months	_____	_____
_____	9 months	_____	_____
_____	10 month	_____	_____
_____	11 months	_____	_____
_____	12 months	_____	_____

Watch me grow

My blood type is _____

My first visits to the doctor_____

_____

_____

_____

How mummy and daddy kept me calm at the doctors

_____

_____

_____

_____

_____

Watch me grow

I first had solid foods was when I was_____old.
My favourite foods were_____
_____
_____
I first fed myself when I was_____ old.
What mummy and daddy did to get me to eat my food
_____
_____
_____
_____
Foods I didn't really like_____
_____
_____
_____
_____

Watch me grow

A picture of me eating

Some funny memories of me with my food_____

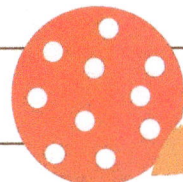

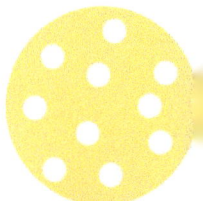

_____

_____

_____

_____

_____

Watch me grow

A picture of me sleeping

I used to wake up _____ times a night.

I first slept through the night when I was _____ old.

Thoughts of mummy and daddy when they see me sleeping_____

_____

_____

_____

Watch me grow

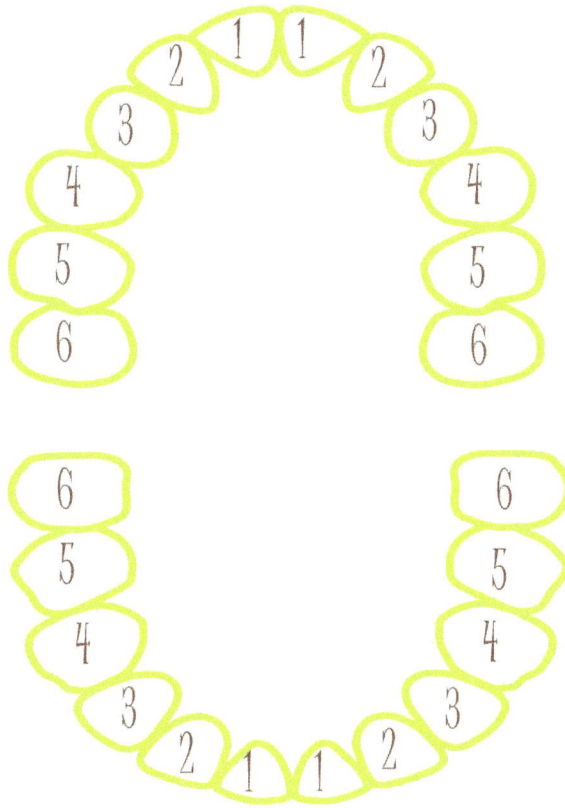

M   D   Y

1.____/____/____

2.____/____/____

3.____/____/____

4.____/____/____

5.____/____/____

6.____/____/____

6.____/____/____

5.____/____/____

4.____/____/____

3.____/____/____

2.____/____/____

1.____/____/____

M   D   Y

____/____/____ .1

____/____/____ .2

____/____/____ .3

____/____/____ .4

____/____/____ .5

____/____/____ .6

____/____/____ .6

____/____/____ .5

____/____/____ .4

____/____/____ .3

____/____/____ .2

____/____/____ .1

My first tooth appeared when I was_____old.

What I was like when I got new teeth_____

_____

_____

_____

My first hair cut

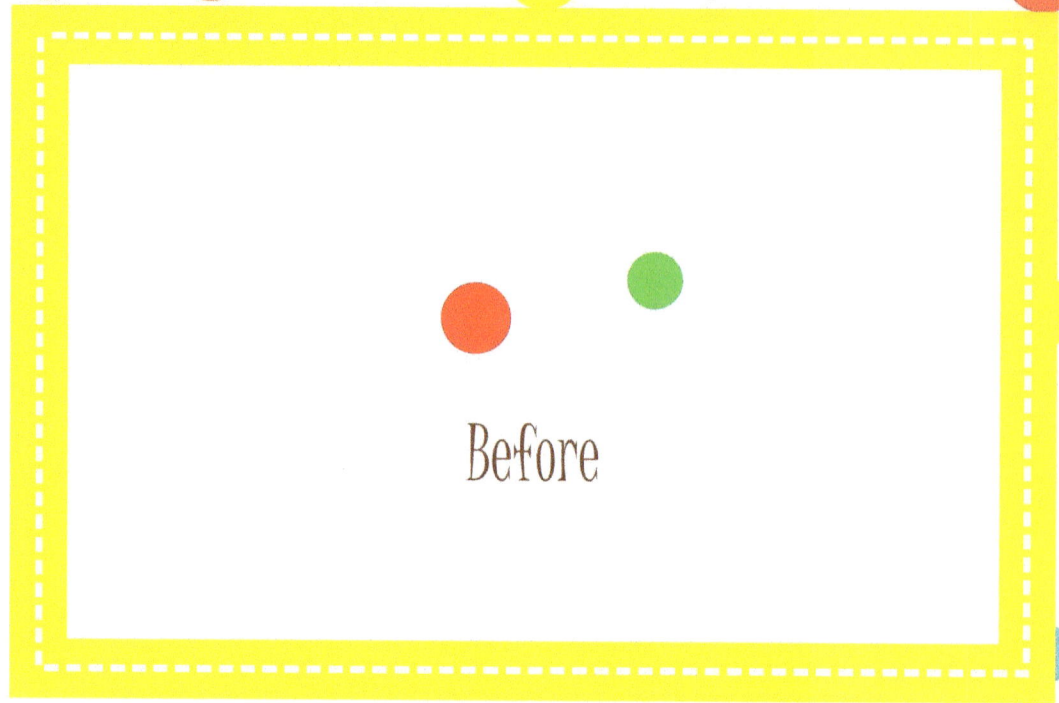

Before

After

Me in the bath

A photo of me in the bath

Date _____

Thoughts _____

_____

_____

_____

Watch me grow

I first smiled when I was _____ old.

The first person I smiled at was _____

I first rolled over when I was _____ old.

The first time I sat by myself I was _____ old.

I first crawled when I was _____ old.

I first stood up by myself when I was _____ old.

The first time I blew a kiss I was _____ old.

The first person I kissed was _____

My first time to walk was when I was _____ old.

I first spoke when I was _____ old.

Some of my first words were _____

_____

_____

_____

_____

_____

Watch me grow

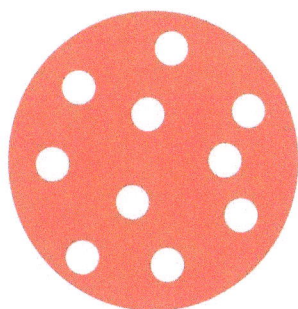

Place photo here

Place photo here

Watch me grow

My favourite colour was_____
My favourite toys were_____
_____

Some of the books I loved to read_____
_____
_____

Some of the things I loved to do_____
_____
_____
_____
_____

My favourite trips outside_____
_____
_____
_____
_____
_____

Watch me grow

Place photo here

Place photo here

My first trips outside

Place photo here

Date_____

Where we went and what we did_____

_____

_____

_____

_____

My first trips outside

The places I loved to go to _____

_____

_____

_____

_____

_____

Mummy and daddy's favourite _____

_____

_____

_____

Watch me grow

Date	Age	Weight	Height
_____	18 months	_____	_____
_____	24 months	_____	_____
_____	2.5 years	_____	_____
_____	3 years	_____	_____
_____	3.5 years	_____	_____
_____	4 years	_____	_____
_____	4.5 years	_____	_____
_____	5 years	_____	_____
_____	5.5 years	_____	_____
_____	6 years	_____	_____
_____	6.5 years	_____	_____
_____	7 years	_____	_____

Watch me grow

The first nursery rhyme I learnt was _____

_____

The first time I learnt all the colours i was _____ old.

I first counted to ten when I was _____ old.

The first time I completed a puzzle by myself I was _____ old.

I first used the potty when I was _____ old.

I first learnt the alphabet when I was _____ old.

Mummy and daddy's favourite memories of teaching me:

_____

_____

_____

_____

_____

_____

My first family holiday

Place photo here

The first holiday I spent with my family was_____

This holiday is special to my family because____

_____

_____

_____

_____

_____

My first family holiday

Place photo here

Date _____

Thoughts_____

_____

_____

_____

_____

_____

_____

My first family adventure

Place photo here

Date _____

Where we went and what we did _____

_____

_____

_____

_____

My first family adventure

Some of my funniest moments _____

_____

_____

_____

_____

_____

Mummy and daddy's favourite memories _____

_____

_____

_____

_____

One year old today

Place photo here

Things I achieved this year_____

_____

_____

Mummy and daddy's thoughts_____

_____

_____

Two years old today

Place photo here

Things I achieved this year_____

_____

_____

Mummy and daddy's thoughts_____

_____

_____

Three years old today

Place photo here

Things I achieved this year_____

_____

_____

Mummy and daddy's thoughts _____

_____

_____

_____

Four years old today

Place photo here

Things I achieved this year _____

_____

_____

_____

Mummy and daddy's thoughts _____

_____

_____

_____

My first day of school

I first started school when I was_____years old.

My first day of school was_____

The colour of my school uniform was_____

I was really excited because_____

_____

What I loved most about school_____

_____

_____

_____

Mummy and daddy's thoughts_____

_____

_____

_____

_____

My first day of school

Place photo here

Place photo here

Special Memories

Place photo here

Thoughts_____

_____

_____

_____

_____

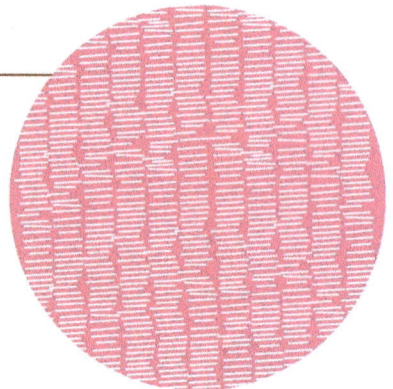

Special memories

Place photo here

Thoughts _____

_____

_____

_____

_____

_____

_____

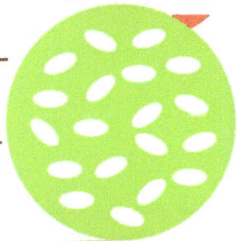
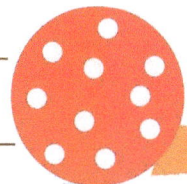

Special Memories

Place photo here

Place photo here

Special Memories

Place photo here

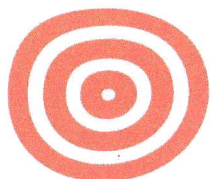

Place photo here

Special memories

Place photo here

Thoughts_____
_____
_____
_____
_____

Special memories

Place photo here

Place photo here

The days go by quickly but I
will cherish each moment I
shared with you forever.
You will always be sunshine.

www.ingramcontent.com/pod-product-compliance
Lightning Source LLC
Chambersburg PA
CBHW040302100426
42811CB00011B/1336